AUSTRALIAN
RAINFORESTS

Photography by Ken Stepnell
Text by Dalys Newman

WOOLLAHRA

PREVIOUS PAGE: Tree ferns form a verdant layer in Tasmanian rainforest. Many fern species grow around the waterways and as the terrain rises, communities of myrtle beech, sassafras, native laurel and celery-top pine are found in the rainforests of Tasmania. Australian tree ferns are all species of *Cyathea* or *Dicksonia*.

ABOVE: Moss-covered rocks in the King River, Tasmania. Water is the common feature of all rainforests—there must be a rainfall of over 1300 millimetres a year to sustain this type of vegetation.

BELOW LEFT: Lake Pedder in Tasmania, an extensive artificial lake and focal point of the Southwest National Park.

BELOW RIGHT: Rich, ferny understoreys, with tree ferns prominent, are features of temperate rainforest, which is widespread in Tasmania and found at all altitudes from sea level to about 1300 metres.

OPPOSITE: Liffy Falls, near Deloraine in Tasmania, are a spectacular example of the many beautiful waterfalls found in the rainforests of this State.

OPPOSITE: A stand of old tree ferns and moss-covered tree trunks in the Mt Field National Park, Tasmania, a region of forests, waterfalls, wild moorland and rugged mountain ranges.

ABOVE: Spectacular Russell Falls, set in a forest of lofty eucalypts in the Mt Field National Park, cascade in two stages into cool shady gorges blanketed with tree ferns.

CENTRE: Roadside waterfall near Queenstown, Tasmania. Temperate rainforest is particularly luxuriant on the west coast of Tasmania because of the high rainfall all year round.

RIGHT: Dove Lake in the Cradle Mountain–Lake St Clair National Park, Tasmania. This area has dense forests of deciduous beech, Tasmanian myrtle, pencil and King Billy pine with an undergrowth of mosses and ferns. Tasmania's most famous park, it encompasses an area of 131 915 hectares.

ABOVE, ABOVE RIGHT AND RIGHT: Towering forests of mountain ash on protected slopes and gullies of myrtle beech rainforest with thick undergrowths of mosses and tree ferns are features of the Maits Rest Walk and Melba Gully in the Otway National Park in Victoria. This cool temperate rainforest area, characterised by a single tree species in the canopy and several species at lower levels, is one of the wettest places in Victoria.

OPPOSITE: Triplet Falls, tumbling in three stages through the bush, are one of the many waterfalls found in the steep slopes and tall forests of the Otway Ranges which merge with the Southern Ocean to form a 12 876 hectare national park in Victoria.

OVERLEAF: The Otway Ranges were formed over 150 million years ago when the great southern landmass known as Gondwanaland began to break up. Ferns, mosses and liverworts were the main form of vegetation in these early days. Tall forests now clothe much of the ranges.

ABOVE: The 18-kilometre Turtons Track in the Otways, Victoria, meanders through fern glades and rainforest, lined by giant messmates and beeches. The original track was cut through this area of bushland in the 1860s.

ABOVE RIGHT: Old tree ferns make a statement at Barnham River in the Otways, Victoria. Favouring moist gullies, tree ferns often form large stands in rainforest areas, their bright green crowns contrasting with their dark stems or trunks, which are covered with fibrous roots. They are impressive relics of the vast fern forests of the Carboniferous period, which occurred more than 250 million years ago.

CENTRE RIGHT: Winter fog shrouds the ferns and mountain ash in the Otways, Victoria.

RIGHT: Majestic old ferns frame the deep red flowers of a Gippsland waratah in a warm temperate rainforest area in the Lind National Park, Victoria. Rainforests provide one of the richest habitats for primitive flowering plants. The familiar plants of the Australian bush—hakeas, grevilleas, banksias and eucalypts—are thought to have evolved from the ancient forests.

LEFT: Warm temperate rainforest in the Lind National Park, East Gippsland, Victoria. This type of rainforest supports trees such as coachwood, crabapple, sassafras, callicoma, lillypilly and corkwood. Temperate rainforests lack the complexity of structure and composition of the subtropical rainforests, being characterised by a rich ferny understorey, an absence of climbers and by a simple one-layer canopy, without emergent trees. The canopy is lower and of a more uniform height. Generally, they are found on less fertile soils and more exposed sites than subtropical forests.

BELOW: Rainforest in the Tarra-Bulga National Park, Gippsland, Victoria. Well-known for its giant mountain ashes, stunning fern gullies and ancient myrtle beeches, this park covers 1625 hectares of original cool temperate rainforest on the Strzelecki Ranges.

OPPOSITE: Ancient tree ferns in the Tarra-Bulga National Park, Gippsland, Victoria. In the temperate rainforest, where palms generally do not grow, their place in the forest structure is taken by tree ferns.

RIGHT: Massed tree ferns, Tarra-Bulga National Park, Victoria. Many ferns soften the landscape of temperate forests, with probably the greatest number of species being found in the fern gullies of the Victorian forests.

BELOW AND CENTRE RIGHT: Cool temperate rainforest at Melba Gully, near Lavers Hill, Victoria. The gully is densely clothed in myrtle beech, blackwood and tree ferns with a lush understorey of mosses and ferns. An interpretive walk explores the forest surrounds.

BOTTOM RIGHT: Rainforest near Cape Otway, just off the Great Ocean Road. Rainforest in south-eastern Australia is found only on the sheltered eastern slopes, in 'wind shadow', as the prevailing winter wind comes from the west and is extremely dry.

OPPOSITE: Moss blankets the damp rocks of the Grey River, off the Great Ocean Road, Victoria. The mosses, lichens and liverworts that cover permanently damp patches of rainforest all play a part in the ecology of this habitat, returning water to the atmosphere and providing humus for other rainforest organisms.

ABOVE: Ferns line the Lilly Pilly Gully walk in the Wilsons Promontory National Park in Victoria. The park has diverse vegetation communities including both cool and warm temperate rainforest.

BELOW: The tree-lined road en route to Mt Erica, Gippsland, Victoria. Erica, an historic mountain timber town, still has one of its original timber mills in operation. Timber-milling has been a constant threat to Australia's rainforests.

ABOVE AND OPPOSITE: Subtropical rainforest along the Great Escarpment at Dorrigo National Park in New South Wales. This type of rainforest is characterised by a profusion of plant forms, large trees, woody lianes and a relatively rich ferny and shrubby understorey. It differs from tropical rainforest in that the canopy trees are at a lower level, thus letting in more light and encouraging thicker vegetation. Subtropical rainforest occurs in patches right down the east coast from the mountains behind Mossman in Queensland to the coastal gullies in the Illawarra district south of Sydney.

CENTRE AND LEFT: Buttressed trunks, strangler figs, rope-like lianes, palms, ferns, mosses and orchids smother every square centimetre of available surface of subtropical rainforest areas. Dorrigo National Park is one of Australia's most accessible World Heritage subtropical rainforests.

LEFT: An understorey of palms creates a luxuriant atmosphere in subtropical rainforest at Port Macquarie, New South Wales. The bangalow or piccabeen palm *(Archontophoenix cunninghamiana)* grows to 30 metres high in rainforest from tropical Queensland to sub-tropical New South Wales. Its feathery head may often be seen stretching above the canopy.

BELOW: The eclectus parrot *(Eclectus roratus)* feeds on the seeds, fruits and flowers of the rainforest canopy in the Cape York Peninsula area. The colouration of the sexes is very different, with the scarlet and blue female being the more vibrant of the species. During courtship there is mutual preening, with the male offering the female tasty tidbits.

ABOVE: Largest of Australia's frogs, the white-lipped tree frog *(Litoria infrafrenta)* is found in the rainforests of tropical Queensland. Averaging about 11 centimetres, it may be green or brown with a distinctive white stripe around the lower lip extending as far back as the shoulders.

ABOVE LEFT: The dainty yellowfoot or wineglass fungus *(Microporus xanthopus)* is common throughout rainforest areas of northern Australia. Its common name refers to the yellow coloured disc that attaches the fruiting body to twigs and branches.

CENTRE LEFT: Lilac fungus *(Hygrophorus lewellinae)* is found on the ground and in leaf litter in the rainforests of south-eastern Australia and Tasmania.

LEFT: A type of bracket fungi, golden leather fungus *(Stereum fasciatum)* is found growing on trees and fallen tree trunks in rainforest areas. Fungi have no green chlorophyll and live by feeding on other things. A bewildering array of fungi are found on rainforest trees and the rich, moist forest floor.

LEFT: The rufous bettong *(Aepyprymnus rufescens)* is found in areas of Victoria, New South Wales and Queensland, including rainforest habitats. It is a very small species of wallaby, weighing about 3 kilograms and reaching 30 centimetres in height.

LEFT: An endangered species, the northern bettong *(Bettongia tropica)* feeds on the fruiting bodies of fungi. Nocturnal, they are solitary animals spending the day hidden in nests concealed in vegetation or leaf litter on the ground.

LEFT: Native to tropical Queensland, the Cooktown orchid *(Dendrobium bigibbum)* is commonly seen forming clumps on trees or rocks in coastal rainforest and monsoon forest. Queensland's floral emblem, this orchid is variable in colour, ranging from white through to light pink or blue to deep pinkish purple. There are about 60 species of dendrobiums native to Australia. Epiphytes, plants that perch on or adhere to other plants, are one of the most characteristic plant groups of the tropical rainforest. There is an enormous variety of epiphytes ranging from mosses and lichens to orchids and giant staghorn ferns.

LEFT: Rainforest dissected by fresh mountain streams is a feature of the heritage listed Springbrook National Park, Queensland. This 2954 hectare park preserves rainforest and eucalypt forest in cliff-lined headwaters of rivers and creeks flowing to the Gold Coast.

OPPOSITE: Purlingbrook Falls plunge over 100 metres into the gully below in Springbrook National Park, south of Brisbane. The area averages 3000 milli-metres of rain per annum, most of which falls between December and March.

OPPOSITE: Abundant rainfall has given rise to a labyrinth of creeks which have carved spectacular waterfalls and deep gorges in the volcanic rocks of Springwood National Park. This area is a remnant of a once huge volcano that last erupted over 22 million years ago. Rich volcanic soils and high rainfall have created a lush subtropical rainforest.

RIGHT: Rainforest pockets dotted throughout Fraser Island in Queensland are dense with huge kauri, rough-barked satinay, brush box and hundreds of airy piccabeen palms. The island was heavily logged during the 20th century but the timber industry ceased in 1992 when it attained World Heritage listing.

RIGHT: A breathtaking suspension bridge takes visitors through the rainforest canopy at O'Reilly's Mountain Resort in the Lamington National Park, Queensland.

RIGHT: Palms and ferns create a diverse understorey in rainforest areas. Although palms seem most appropriate to the tropics and ferns to cooler climates, species of both occur in all types of rainforest. The most noticeable difference in the forests of the north and south is the reduction in the number of tree species and the density of the canopy in the cooler rainforests, with an increase in the ferny, shrubby understorey.

OVERLEAF: High humidity that results from mist favours the growth of cool temperate forest in Lamington National Park, Queensland.

ABOVE: Millstream Falls, the widest falls in Australia, spill over an old basalt lava flow. The dry open woodland vegetation here, in the rain shadow of the eastern dividing ranges, offers a stark contrast to the dense rainforest only a few kilometres away. Variability in rainfall is one of the major factors determining vegetation type. Generally, a yearly average rainfall above 1300 millimetres is needed to support subtropical and warm temperate rainforest and at least 1750 millimetres for cool temperate rainforest.

BELOW LEFT: Rainforest on the Atherton Tablelands in tropical northern Queensland. Tropical rainforest is overwhelming in its complexity of plant and animal life.

BELOW RIGHT: The McHugh Bridge spans the Beatrice River in the Palmerston North National Park, Queensland. Situated 125 kilometres south of Cairns, this is an area of high, dense rainforest, deep gorges, rivers, waterfalls and abundant birdlife.

OPPOSITE: Queensland's tropical rainforests are rich with luxuriant growth, featuring tangled arrays of vines and climbers.

OPPOSITE: Tropical rainforest in Queensland's Innisfail district. This type of rainforest consists of three to five layers, forming a closed canopy that blocks off most of the light to the lower strata.

ABOVE: The Beatrice River flows through tropical rainforest in the Palmerston National Park, north Queensland. Tall solitary trees, emerging from the dense canopy below, are a feature of this type of rainforest.

CENTRE RIGHT: Rainforest bushland in the Palmerston National Park. Treelets and shrubs below 5 metres in height make up the shrub layer of tropical rainforests, and the ground layer nurtures herbs, ferns, seedlings and fungi.

BOTTOM RIGHT: Tropical rainforest is characterised by a 'clean' forest floor and the presence of epiphytes, lianes, and deep green, broad-leaved plants.

ABOVE: Fertile volcanic soils and the variability of rainfall in the 20 200 hectare Lamington National Park in Queensland yield a lush environment of diverse vegetation including mist-shrouded cool temperate rainforest and the largest preserved stand of subtropical rainforest in Australia.

CENTRE LEFT: Rainforest in the Daintree area of northern Queensland. A tangled under-growth of plants, such as stinging nettle and lantana, forms beneath any gaps in the canopy of the tropical rainforest.

BOTTOM LEFT: Graceful, lacy false bracken (Calochaena dubia) thrives in moist rainforest environments, often colonising hillsides where there is filtered light.

OPPOSITE: Copperlode dam in northern Queensland lies within the wet tropics, a dis-continuous area of forested land extending 450 kilometres between Townsville and Cairns. The most luxuriant, complex and diverse of all plant communities, this type of rainforest once covered much of the conti-nent. This area was declared a World Heritage site in 1988.

LEFT: Fluted trunks, buttresses and surface roots characterise many rainforest trees. They provide a safeguard against severe storms and help the tree acquire nutrients from the often shallow forest soil. This type of growth occurs in members of many tree families and their gnarled bases, sometimes tinged green with moss, give a fairyland quality to the forest.

BELOW: Rainforest in the Daintree area of northern Queensland. Australia is fortunate in possessing some beautiful remnants of relatively undisturbed rainforest with its diverse range of plants and animals, but in the past 200 years of settlement half of Australia's rainforest has disappeared due to commercial and residential exploitation. In 1981 the Australian Conservation Foundation accorded rainforests major priority status and much has since been achieved in the protection of these unique ecosystems.